Reflections on Learning

REFLECTIONS

ON LEARNING

Howard Mumford Jones

Essay Index Reprint Series

BOOKS FOR LIBRARIES PRESS

FREEPORT, NEW YORK

Copyright © 1958 by Rutgers,
The State University
Reprinted 1969 by arrangement with
Rutgers University Press

STANDARD BOOK NUMBER:
8369-0022-7

LIBRARY OF CONGRESS CATALOG CARD NUMBER:
69-17580

MANUFACTURED
BY
HALLMARK LITHOGRAPHERS, INC.
IN THE U.S.A.

FOR WHITNEY J. OATES

The 1958 Brown and Haley Lectures are the sixth of a series given annually at the College of Puget Sound, Tacoma, Washington, by a scholar distinguished for his work in Social Studies or the Humanities. The purpose of these lectures is to present original analyses of some intellectual problems confronting the present age.

Preface

These lectures are not intended to present a complete theory of humanistic scholarship or of aesthetic judgment or of education in America. They are in part a protest against an obsession with practicality, in part an examination of a number of pedagogical theories about the arts in education, and in part a rapid review of humanistic scholarship, ending with a plea for a fusion of the point of view of the scholar, the point of view of the critic, and the point of view of the artist. The function of these lectures is to be suggestive, not dogmatic.

Their publication creates a curious and amusing difficulty about tenses. When I was working on them, the President of the United States delivered the two messages, the implication of which forms no small part of my early remarks; and when I delivered the lectures, the Congress was still considering the appropriation bills. By the time this book is put into circulation, we shall know what disposition has been made of the recommendations from the White House. After some thought, I have resolved to keep my original tenses in discussing the possibilities latent in the two documents I analyze and ask the reader charitably to put himself backward in time to the April evenings of 1958 when I delivered these lectures on the campus of the College of Puget Sound in Tacoma, Washington.

Like my predecessors in the Brown and Haley lectureship I had a wonderful time in Tacoma.

—Howard Mumford Jones
Cambridge, Massachusetts,
May 9, 1958

Contents

1 *War, Science, and Learning*

It is a mark of the restlessness of our age that since receiving the kind invitation to deliver these lectures, I have had to reconsider the basis of their organization three times. I had originally intended to inquire into the relation to what we used to call culture, of the charge that Johnny can't read. The fact that the Modern Language Association of America is currently inquiring into the implications of Johnny's inability to read Spanish or French or German, despite expensive efforts to

make him do so, seemed to me to have large implications. I still think the implications are startling.
But this simpler problem has disappeared into
graver issues. The first of these arose from the
passionate excitement created by our discovery that
the Russians had launched two artificial satellites
and we had launched none. Instead of sending a
courteous message of congratulation upon a no-
table scientific achievement, as the Russians were
to do when we got our own up past the strato-
sphere, we jumped to the conclusion that American
science is a failure, American education a fraud,
American defense leaders incompetent, and an
invasion from Mars or Siberia imminent. At all
costs we must have scientists and engineers. But
how we can best educate scientists and engineers,
or whether we need a gross additional quantity
of scientists and engineers half as much as we
need unfettered, imaginative scientists and engineers—these more complex questions, at once
philosophic and practical, we refused to consider.

Macaulay once wrote of the British public in
a seven-year fit of morality. We in this country
have our seven-year fits also, especially about problems of education. Instead of giving education

our steady and respectful attention as a chief means of continuing American culture, we forget all about it for months on end; and then when a sputnik comes along or New York City finds it has criminals in its classrooms, we seize a stick and begin laying about us mightily.

Then in January, 1958, we read, first, the President's budget message and, second, his message on education, both of which, if I may say so without disrespect, show powerful traces of our emotional debauch. If the principal suggestions about education in these documents are carried out—and some of them will be—I, for one, regard the two messages, taken together, as one of the most fateful documents in American educational history: a dual document at least as crucial as the Morrill Act of 1862, which in the guise of giving public land to agricultural and engineering colleges, in the sequel established military training as part of education in the liberal arts. To the implication of these messages I shall come in a moment.

I have, however, clung to my original title—*Reflections on Learning.* Since my allusion to Johnny's illiteracy seems to refer to the grade schools, it may be surmised that I am going to discuss the learning process in school, that vast topic which fascinates biologists, parents, teachers, policemen, and professors of educational psychology. The learning I have in mind is not of this sort. By learning I shall mean humane learning— that is, knowledge of and about the humanities. By the humanities I mean literature and the languages, philosophy, ethics, logic, religion (but not religion in a sectarian sense and not formal theology), the fine arts and their history, music and its history, the theory of architecture philosophically taken, and, indeed, general history. History has important connections with social science, for example, in the case of anthropology; but the social sciences have important connections with the humanities, for example, in the matter of values and value judgments. I shall continue to claim history as a humanity. We are, however, in a region wherein exact demarcation is difficult. I have even heard claims that the central humanity is no longer philosophy but modern psychology—especially, I take it, in view of the gloomy nature of contemporary fiction, modern clinical psychology.

More important is it to distinguish between knowledge *of* and knowledge *about* the humanities.

The distinction is not valid for the whole subject, but it is valid in the arts. Clearly we may have knowledge *of* an art and knowledge *about* an art. Some regard knowledge *about* any art, especially if it be knowledge of a traditional or conventional sort, as destructive of originality and imagination; but there are also devotees of knowledge *about* the arts who look with scorn on those who practice them, especially in public or if they earn a living by so doing. Thus a school which teaches commercial art is commonly excluded from the humane world, whereas a department of music which teaches musical theory and musical history but not musical performance is never excluded from *our* church. This may be called the high and dry theory of the humanities. The problem is real, but its solution is seldom realistic. For example, English departments offer composition courses which permit students to write fiction, but they do not train them to write what I may call commercial fiction. Departments of drama commonly produce plays, but they do not commonly maintain schools of acting in the professional sense; and departments of fine arts, though they offer instruction in painting and drawing, do not offer instruction in profitable painting and drawing. Obviously this problem does not come up in departments of philosophy, history, or religion.

Humane learning is now one-third of organized knowledge outside theology. The other two provinces are the sciences and the social sciences. The relations among these branches of knowledge have fluctuated. In the Middle Ages all secular lore was subordinate to theology and was divided into two divisions, not three. One of these—the trivium, comprising grammar, rhetoric, and logic—had to do with the expression of thought; and the other—the quadrivium, comprising arithmetic, geometry, astronomy, and music—had to do with science, or, if you prefer, mathematics. Weary of ecclesiastical domination, Renaissance scholars in their turn split knowledge still another way: into theology, or knowledge of God; and humanism, or secular knowledge created by and about man. Humanism was supposed to show what man, unaided by providence, could accomplish. Its central discipline was philosophy as distinguished from theology, though it was understood that philosophic ideas were not thereby denied to theologians, nor were arguments about the being of God denied to philosophers. As time went on, secular philosophy devoted more and more attention to knowledge of the world in which man lives, that is, to natural philosophy, the mother of modern science. Science finally broke away from humanism during the seventeenth century when the experimental method had thoroughly proved itself, although chairs of natural philosophy continued into the nineteenth century. The independence of the social sciences began in the eighteenth century when, in 1776, Adam Smith in *The Wealth of Nations* laid the groundwork of modern economic theory. Humanism is no longer an earthly god, the humanities are now but one part in three of the total realm of secular knowledge; but humanism and the humanities are, it is clear, one of the oldest of man's creations.

If I refer to the several parts of knowledge as being on a theoretical equality, I refer not so much to the distribution of student hours or of faculty budgets or of popular understanding and misunderstanding of education as I do to the philosophy of American culture. Far from arguing that the diminished empire of the humanities proves that their effective life is over, scientists and social scientists of repute have said precisely the opposite.

They have said that the humanities should be more richly taught and more widely distributed among our people than ever before, for the reason that they are crucial to the good life in an industrialized technological society. If somebody charges that science and the social sciences are "inhumane," the scientists and the social scientists bristle with indignation. Even if some among them argue that anthropology or physics or biology or social psychology is in the twentieth century a central element in humanism, they do not deny the validity to our culture of music, the fine arts, literature, philosophy, religion, ethics, and history.

The doctrine of intellectual equality among the three great divisions of knowledge prevailed up to World War I. It was the governing concept both for secondary education and for higher education. It took form as liberal education, and liberal education as a matter of course exposed the student to each of the three parts of knowledge before permitting him to specialize in any part of any one of them. Even today, in the guise of general education, most colleges and some high schools are struggling to retain balance among the three divisions. Unfortunately the theoretical balance has more recently been so overweighted on one side, it can scarcely be said to exist. Why?

Scientists are not to blame, but perhaps statesmen are. The American Civil War, sometimes called the first modern war, saw the increased participation of scientists and engineers in armed conflict, notably in the creation and use of such inventions as the observation balloon, booby traps, the ironclad, the use of railroads for logistic purposes, the electric telegraph, and improved fire control. Partly as a consequence, the number of reputable engineering colleges in the country increased from six at the time of Gettysburg to one hundred forty-eight when the depression of 1929 began. Partly also as a consequence the government created the National Academy of Sciences in 1863. World War I was even more scientific, involving tanks, new medical inventions, poison gas, the use of radio, magnetic mines, new submarines, the airplane, and so on. Inevitably, therefore, the National Academy of Sciences offered to set up a National Research Council to aid the government. President Wilson accepted this offer; the Council was made permanent in 1918 and reorganized in 1919. It is still functioning. The companionship of science, engineering, and destruction was even closer in World War II, which saw the employment of radar, loran, airplane carriers, new forms of mines, new forms of rockets, and, eventually, the atom bomb. The National Science Board recommended, and Congress created in 1950, the National Science Foundation largely for purposes of defense. No body similar to any of these several scientific bodies has, so far as I am aware, ever been created on analogous lines by the Federal government for the humanities. The original appropriation for the National Science Foundation was $225,000. In 1956 this appropriation had been increased seventy times and reached $16 million, but the 1958 budget message proposed to give the Foundation $58 million for research and $82 million for science education, or $140 million in all, a sum more than 622 times the money given this body eight years earlier. This figure of course does not include other money to be appropriated for scientific work in other areas of the government. The cost of institutions like the Library of Congress and the National Museum of Art is in comparison negligible; and the amount of money appropriated, or recommended to be appropriated directly, by the government for research and education in the humanities is zero dollars.

Let us remember that the Federal budget is not the product of a single man. It is an ordering by the Bureau of the Budget of the infinite requests for money that pour in upon it, together with a plan for financing any new policies a given administration would like to see adopted. I suspect that no matter who was in the White House, the budget message, given the political situation, would not have differed greatly from that of Mr. Eisenhower. Whatever one may think of our foreign policies, I therefore propose to treat the budget message as a public document, not as a partisan document. It shows the way we have been going for a very long time. I do not like what I see in that document and what I am compelled to infer from it, about American education; and I shall explain why. But I am not concerned with Mr. Eisenhower or his cabinet or his party; I am concerned with the implications of tendencies only too evident, for the future of American culture.

Science would seem to be faring rather well. Nevertheless, in 1956 the Chairman of the National Science Board insisted that "the scarcity of trained scientists is acute." His opinion echoes in the President's so-called message on education of January 27, 1958. Nine-tenths of the emphasis in that message is laid on education in science and engineering. Everything else is treated in the vaguest general terms, except for foreign languages.

But let me turn back to the budget message of 1958. It asked for appropriations totaling about $74 billion. Of this enormous sum $46 billion or 62 per cent was for national security. In 1950 we spent about $13 billion on national security; in 1958 we were asked to increase this amount by about 350 per cent. The total budget for 1950 was a little over $39.5 billion; the total budget proposed for 1958 was a little less than $74 billion, an increase of about 87 per cent. The increases proposed in the area of national security, it is clear, bear no relation to the general increase in the budget. The increase in 1958 over 1950 in sums suggested for education mainly in science is an increase of about 650 per cent, an increase 300 per cent greater than the percentage increase for even our total national security. This vast increase, I repeat, is for education in science and engineering; every other area

of education except for fleeting references to foreign languages is hurried over. Foreign languages
are there, it is obvious, not for their cultural
import but as part of our national defense plan.

The enormous increase in the amounts asked
for in the field of scientific education and research does not come about from the pure, Platonic
love of knowledge. It is motivated by fear of Russia
—a country where in 1931 as sympathetic an ob-
server as Professor George S. Counts found freedom of research "considerably curtailed" and the
entire educational system dedicated to the proposition that the Soviet state is an earthly god that
can do no wrong. That country, operating under
this ideal, has now caught up with us and threatens
to surpass us, and the way to meet this "challenge"
according to the budget message is to produce an
ever "growing supply of highly trained man-power
—scientists, engineers, teachers, and technicians."
"Teachers" in this context mean teachers of science
and mathematics and perhaps of foreign languages.

In order to create or employ this growing supply of highly trained man-power the budget proposed increases in funds for the Atomic Energy

Commission, the National Advisory Committee for Aeronautics, the Department of Defense, the Bureau of Standards, and the National Institute of Health. But the emphasis was upon the appropriation suggested for the National Science Foundation and for the Department of Health, Education and Welfare in the matter of education. Let us look at these proposals. I shall for this purpose combine information from the budget message and information from the education message, which parallels the budget message and amplifies the details of the program proposed for education.

The appropriation proposed for the National Science Foundation in its educational activities is $82 million, a fivefold increase over the previous sum for this purpose. The National Science Foundation directly initiates programs in the teaching of science and mathematics. But the appropriation proposed for the Department of Health, Education and Welfare in this regard is one of matching dollars—that is, for every dollar appropriated by a state or local educational authority in fields agreeable to the Federal government, that government will pay out another dollar. Programs include testing of pupillary ability in science; strengthening of guidance services; a program for fellowship aid tagged with the direction that "reasonable preference should be given students with good preparation or high aptitude in science or mathematics"; money for additional teachers of science and mathematics and for laboratory equipment; and, in higher education, graduate fellowships in general but, more specifically, support of special centers and institutes for foreign language study—"it is important to our national security," says the message, to have our deficiencies in foreign languages "promptly overcome." This is an "emergency" program of four years. One can only trust that enough persons will become fluent in Chinese, Russian, Arabic, Hebrew, German, and other foreign languages in this interval. Meanwhile the National Science Foundation is of its own initiative to interest able high school students in scientific careers, improve methods of teaching and the contents of courses in mathematics and science, offer supplementary training (in summer institutes, for example) to teachers of science, and provide fellowships for qualified college graduates and scientists for advanced study in science and mathematics.*

We read in the budget message that "the basic responsibility for science education and training as well as for the conduct of research . . . depends on 'non-Federal support," and that this program must "be considered as an emergency stimulant to encourage the states and local communities to bring their educational systems up to date in the light of our modern scientific age." We read also that "national needs require the development through a strong general educational system of a vast number of attitudes and skills."

* These lectures were delivered in March, 1958. Late in August of that year the Congress passed the bill giving Federal aid to education. This appropriated $887 million. It substituted student loans for student scholarships and kept the provision requiring special consideration for students in science, mathematics, and the modern foreign languages. It appropriated $280 million on a dollar-for-dollar "matching" basis for equipment in mathematics, science, and the foreign languages. It included $7¼ million for institutes for teachers of modern foreign languages, and $8 million for exploring "little known" languages—that is, little known in the United States—$15 million of aid in vocational education, and $18 million for research in educational television. There is a vague tincture of the humanities in the provisions for improving teaching in the languages, but in general the measure as passed exhibits the philosophy set forth in the Presidential message which helped to shape it. As I am interested in tendencies rather than in bookkeeping, I have therefore kept the text as I uttered it.

This is an admirable sentiment, but the only attitudes or skills the Federal government is prepared to pay for under the scheme is skill in science and technology and skill in foreign languages for utilitarian purposes; and I, for one, am unable to reconcile these vague phrases about the desirability of developing a vast number of attitudes and skills needed by the country, with the enormous increase suggested for the National Science Foundation to develop only one type of skill. Nor is the dilemma solved by calling this an emergency program or by referring the problem back to the local or state educational authorities. However lofty the desires of the local school board or the state superintendents of public instruction to maintain balance in education, they must face the fact that during four years, for every dollar they spend for the school library or school music or school art, the Federal government would give nothing at all; but for every dollar they spend on laboratory equipment or science testing or something of that sort, the Federal government would give them an extra dollar. In sum, it would cost them 50 per cent less to teach science than it would to teach almost any other subject. Finally, the teacher of science, if he is any good at all, would get help of all sorts, including pleasant summer institutes; but if the English teacher or the history teacher or the art teacher or the music teacher wants professional advancement, he or she would have to pay to go to a summer school, or have the way paid by the local board, a charge that inevitably increases the cost of teaching nonscientific subjects.

The Report of the Carnegie Foundation for the Advancement of Teaching of 1956–1957 is a fair-minded discussion of Federal aid in American education; but I have been pondering, ever since I read the budget message of 1958, a remark of an eminent educator quoted in the Report, who described the National Science Foundation as the perfect formula for producing a legislated imbalance in higher education. Under the budget scheme as proposed this imbalance would now overtake secondary education. As for the term "temporary" attached to this program, I have seen too much temporary housing year after year in Washington to gloss the word in anything but a Pickwickian sense.

The vast dislocation of traditional educational values envisaged in the budget message of 1958 as a temporary dislocation is temporary only in the sense that until it is accepted by local authorities the Federal government would foot the bill; but after that, so far as I can make out, it will be the principal purpose of our schools to produce scientists and engineers. At least, I see nothing in either document about producing a "growing supply of highly trained man-power" in the ministry, or the arts, or law, or music, or social service, or farming, or salesmanship, or sports, or any other customary American folkway. The single, central demand is for scientists and engineers. This demand arises, not from any hope that the secret of the universe is about to be discovered by disinterested scientists, but from scare.

There is an ancient Roman apothegm which runs that in the midst of war the laws are silent —one of those half-truths for which the Romans were notorious. On the same line it is sometimes argued that when the country is in peril, criticism should cease. I do not myself see that the country is in any such degree of peril as the more timid among us suppose, but let us for the moment all agree that the country is in peril. I have the normal dislike of dying, and I have a healthy desire to have my country survive, provided that what survives is something I can recognize as my country and not some transformed political entity. I am not skilled in military matters or in international affairs, but we have those among us who are. Let us put the question to them. What will happen to the nation we have known and loved, the way of life we have liked, the values we have cherished, what we vaguely call the American dream—and to the fulfillment of this dream our educational system, however imperfect, has been dedicated—what will happen to the United States if we go all out for science and engineering for military purposes?

I turn, first of all, to General Omar N. Bradley, whose integrity is unquestioned, whose military experience one can follow in his book, *A Soldier's Story,* and whose speech at St. Alban's School near Washington last November should give us pause. Here is the first paragraph:

"The central problem of our time—as I view it —is how to employ human intelligence for the salvation of mankind. It is a problem we have put upon ourselves. For we have defiled our intellect by the creation of such scientific instruments of destruction that we are now in desperate danger of destroying ourselves. Our plight is critical and with each effort we have made to relieve it by further scientific advance, we have succeeded only in aggravating our peril. As a result, we are now speeding inexorably toward a day when even the ingenuity of our scientists may be unable to save us from the consequences of a single rash act or a lone reckless hand upon the switch of an uninterceptible missile. For twelve years now we've sought to stave off disaster by devising arms which would be both ultimate and disastrous." The time will come, at this rate, he said, when we can do no more than attempt to "smother our fears and attempt to live in a thickening shadow of death." "We can compete with a sputnik," he says a little later, "and probably create bigger and better sputniks of our own. But what are we doing to prevent the sputnik from evolving into just one more weapons system? And when are we going to muster the intelligence equal to that applied against the sputnik and dedicate it to the preservation of this satellite on which we live?"

The problem of peaceful accommodation as between Russia and the United States is, says the General, "infinitely more difficult than the conquest of space, infinitely more complex than a trip to the moon." The instruments that will help us work out this accommodation are, according to him, imagination, reason, and general intelligence. But the emphasis of the budget message and the message on education is not on imagination, reason, and general intelligence; it is on the quick production of more technologists for purposes of security only.

I turn next to Walter Millis, who has devoted a lifetime to writing about military affairs, and to his article "How to Compete with the Russians," which you will find in *The New York Times Magazine* for February 2, 1958. Mr. Millis asks the same question that General Bradley asks: Is it possible to "defend the American free society" without "destroying its essential freedoms in the process"? Mr. Millis comes up with the same answer that General Bradley gives: If we continue to go about it as we are now going about it, the answer is: No. Why? Because, says Mr. Millis, "the nuclear arms race is not reaching the hoped-for climax . . . on the contrary, it is barely beginning." He notes that the atom bomb was born of frantic fear that the Germans might beat us to it; the fact is the Germans "were not even in the race. The race was a fantasy; the bomb, when it appeared, was tragically real." A policy built upon an effort to keep ahead of the Russians will be, he says, "astronomically expensive"; it will require taxation on such a scale as "must work important transformations in the social and political bases of the economic system," a system in which the aviation industry is "already the single biggest employer in the nation," a system in which government orders are concentrated "in the hands of no more than a dozen big corporations . . . directed by an essentially self-perpetuating managerial elite" moving of necessity farther and farther away from "our conventional concepts of free enterprise and individual liberty."

Then comes a passage so powerfully expressed I must quote it as a whole: "Any society which pins its hope of survival upon its technical ability to massacre scores of millions of the enemy's innocent non-combatants, which is at the same time reckless of its responsibility for poisoning, in the name of self-defense, the atmosphere and food-bearing soil of the whole earth has accepted a moral degradation which denies it any title to

freedom within itself. It has accepted a brutaliza-
tion of its foreign policy which must inevitably
brutalize and poison its internal life as well." Such
a policy denies or disregards "those fundamental
concepts of the inherent value of the individual,
of the dignity and fraternity of all men, of justice
not only for one's self but for all, which many believe to be the indispensable foundation of any
free society." Like General Bradley, Mr. Millis can
see no hope in merely getting more scientists and
engineers to work for the government on weapons
of destruction: A military state cannot also remain
a state in which individual freedoms are maintained as we have known them, and for him as for
General Bradley the only hope is an imaginative,
rational, and intelligent peace. Can you nourish
imagination, reason, and intelligence without the
humanities? I think not.

But let us, being Americans, look on the bright
side. Let us hope for the best. Let us suppose that
these government-subsidized scientists work for
peace and prosperity. What sort of world shall we
have? I turn to the scientists for answer, or rather
to an answer by six distinguished research scien-

tists who were persuaded by this same *New York Times Magazine* to write their thoughts on what the world might be like in A.D. 2057. The group included a geneticist, a rocket expert, two chemists, a biologist, and a psychologist; and their prophecies are preceded by the caution: "provided mankind survives that long." The geneticist, Dr. Herman Muller of Indiana, was happy about the prospects of artificial insemination and of parthenogenesis for the human animal. The rocket expert, Dr. Wernher von Braun, thought that the United States would surround the earth with a whole family of artificial satellites, some of which, "the best money-makers," he says, "will have taken over the mailman's job." Dr. Harrison Scott Brown, professor of geochemistry at California Institute of Technology, looked forward to an age of thermonuclear power but seemed to doubt whether man could develop "the moral, the social and the political means of living with man." President Clifford C. Furnas, of Buffalo, a chemist, was hopeful about biochemistry but shared Dr. Brown's scepticism about mankind. Dr. James Bonner, a biologist at California Institute of Technology,

looked forward to a future of vegetable steaks, "flavored with tasty synthetics and made chewy by
addition of a suitable plastic matrix."

Dr. John Weir, a psychologist at the same institution, hoped to uncover the operations of human
motives, values, feelings, and emotions and so reduce the amount of "malfunctions." But he hoped
also that by 2057 "man should be able to generate
creative ideas at will, simultaneously taking into
account all possible combinations of known varia-
bles." But that is not all he says. I quote him
further:

Principles of dynamic psychology, he writes,
will by then "tell us how to form groups, how to
develop group goals, how to select group leaders,
how to reach effective group decisions. The process
by which an aggregate of people becomes a closely
knit unit, an integrated team will be understood.
This will enable us to make very rapid social
changes, to eliminate the lag in culture, and to
develop desirable social organizations in very short
spans of time." Dr. Weir does not say what he
means by "us" in this context; that is to say, he
does not tell us who is to initiate the process by
which effective group decisions are to eventuate in

an integrated team overcoming social lag by very
rapid changes. Indeed, he fails to define "desirable
social.organizations," "creative ideas," "integrated
team," and a number of other components in this
dream of a happy state. Doubtless he had not
space in a newspaper article, but we can make a
guess at possibilities by simply re-reading either
Mr. Skinner's *Walden II* or Mr. Orwell's *1984*.
And when the reproach is made, as it is always
made in this connection, "Why do you individ-
ualists always assume that the only possible out-
come of psychological conditioning is a robotized
society?" the answer is just as good as the question,
"Why do you psychologists assume anything else?
Who is to condition the conditioners? Who is to
determine whose cultural lag and whose well-inte-
grated group is to disappear or to survive?"

Eating vegetable steaks flavored with tasty synthetics, casually making a date for artificial insemi-
nators to arrive and fertilize his wife, while he
pays government a fee for a fast message from a
highly profitable artificial satellite, the American
of the future, if any Americans survive, will then
stroll off for an hour of creative idea-making, after
which dynamic psychology will take over and inte-

grate him into a group engaged in overcoming cultural lag by making effective group decisions under a group leader. Other group leaders will, I take it, distribute thermonuclear power to the deserving few in a happy republic developing desirable social organizations everywhere in very short spans of time. Somehow it is not thus that I had envisaged the future.

I turn finally to the confession of a scientist who revolutionized thought—to Charles Darwin. Darwin, in response to requests from his children, wrote in his later years an autobiography which is a minor classic of literature. Toward the end of it appears this moving passage: "I have said that in one respect my mind has changed during the last twenty or thirty years. Up to the age of thirty, or beyond it, poetry of many kinds, such as the works of Milton, Gray, Byron, Wordsworth, Coleridge, and Shelley, gave me great pleasure, and even as a schoolboy I took intense delight in Shakespeare, especially in the historical plays. I have also said that formerly pictures gave me considerable, and music very great, delight. But now for many years I cannot endure to read a line of poetry . . . I have also almost lost my taste for pictures or music.

. . . I retain some taste for fine scenery, but it does not cause me the exquisite delight which it formerly did." Novels, he said, he could still read.

He then continues: "This curious and lamentable loss of the higher aesthetic tastes is all the odder, as books on history, biographies, and travels . . . and essays on all sorts of subjects interest me as much as ever they did. My mind seems to have become a kind of machine for grinding general laws out of large collections of facts, but why this should have caused the atrophy of that part of the brain alone, on which the higher tastes depend, I cannot conceive. A man with a mind more highly organised or better constituted than mine, would not, I suppose, have thus suffered; and if I had to live my life again, I would have made a rule to read some poetry and listen to some music at least once every week. . . . The loss of these tastes is a loss of happiness, and may possibly be injurious to the intellect, and more probably to the moral character, by enfeebling the emotional part of our nature."

The loss of these tastes is a loss of happiness, and may possibly be injurious to the intellect, and more probably to the moral character. Such is the pathetic discovery of one of the great scientific philosophers of all time after a life patiently devoted to biology.* What he complains about is precisely the cultural imbalance created, or threatened to be created, by our mistaken assumption that the way to beat the Russians is to lower happiness, injure the intellect, and damage the moral character. Surely a country in which the right to pursue happiness is one of the three enumerated rights singled out by the document that brought it into being has in turn not only the right but the duty to ask of those who are presently shaping its educational future whether the future they envisage is one in which survival will have enough value to make it worth while to have survived. I think there are more parts to learning than science, engineering, and the mastery of foreign languages for purposes of national defense, and to these other parts of learning I shall now come.

* It is sometimes argued that because Darwin is said to have suffered from melancholia in his old age, the statement is untrustworthy. It seems to me the melancholia resulted from the deprivation, and not the other way around.

2 *The Grammar of the Arts*

In the first phase of my argument I analyzed the drive toward making the teaching of science central in American education through giving it enormous financial advantages over the teaching of everything else; I looked at a picture of the future as recently envisaged by half a dozen living scientists at the request of *The New York Times,* and I quoted a great scientist, Charles Darwin, about his sense of loss as, under the pressure of scientific labor, his finer sensibilities decayed for lack of nourishment from the humanities. I said also that in my opinion politicians rather than scientists were primarily responsible for the drive to make scientific and technical education paramount in America. Inasmuch as my remarks may easily be misconstrued as an attack on science as such, let me repeat what I have tried to make clear, namely, that I am not assailing science or attacking statesmen. My interest is in cultural tendencies as they affect or are affected by education. I know too many excellent scientists who sincerely deplore the one-sided education some industrialists would like to force on the country, to believe that intelligent scientists want either to monopolize or to dominate American education.

Moreover, scientists have grounds for complaint. They say that science is not well enough taught in the secondary schools. This situation is created by a multiplicity of factors—poor training of teachers, false theories of educational psychology, failure of school authorities to understand the nature of science, the pressure of industry to get technicians, antiquated textbooks, inadequate laboratories in the secondary schools, theories of teaching which exalt self-expression without regard to exactitude, and so on. Scientists aver that progress in scientific education is retarded because the colleges have perpetually to do over again in the first two years what the high schools failed to do in four.

They do not often say, but they might also say, that because of the fantastic increase of knowledge in every science, the gap between what can be done in the secondary schools and what has to be learned later in order to get on with the scientific enterprise widens every month. Finally, they do say, but they do not say with sufficient emphasis, that science must not be confounded with application or intervention—gadget-making, or hardware.

Science is a way of looking at the world, just as poetry or painting or philosophy is a way of looking at the world. It is a form of interpretation filled with austere grandeur, with beauty on a big and on a little scale, with challenges to intellectual curiosity, with fundamental components of a philosophical and even a religious view of life. The wonder is that scientists have any trouble in recruiting the young. One would have surmised that their problem would be rather that of fending off eager applicants for training. Scientists, it is clear, do not wish to obliterate the arts, or philosophy, or religion, or any other great traditional form of human experience and cultural values. All the scientists want is what seems to them proper equality with the other parts of knowledge.

Certainly science teaching in our secondary schools can be improved, albeit competent reports indicate it is not so bad as excitable reformers make out. But our inferiority in this field is marked when we compare our achievement with that of foreign educational systems. Virtually every American college has to re-teach elementary mathematics, although mathematics is par excellence the supreme analytical instrument of our time. Proposals to meet such deficiencies by modernizing textbooks, or creating refresher courses for teachers, or re-equipping laboratories, or paying young talent to enter a scientific career follow naturally.

Two important questions, however, arise immediately: Is the deficiency of teaching in the secondary schools confined to science? And if it is not, will emphasis upon science teaching automatically result in improved teaching all along the line? The answer to the second question seems to me clear enough: Improvement in the teaching of any subject tends to raise the general level of teaching in any institution, but the tendency is erratic and unpredictable, and may even generate a counter-tendency of despair. But what about the larger issue?

Well, concerning foreign language teaching we have the message of the President of the United States. This teaching is inadequate. Government has had to set up special training programs for the armed forces and for officials and employees in our civil service, since, I am reliably informed, about 75 per cent of those whose posts require a knowledge of some foreign tongue have no competent knowledge whatsoever.

What about history? Inquire of the members of the American Historical Association. Or try such a simple test as asking your friends to name as many presidents as they can between Lincoln and Theodore Roosevelt. If that is too hard, ask them when the Panama Canal opened, or when the popular election of United States Senators became law, or when and where President Franklin D. Roosevelt enunciated the doctrine of the Four Freedoms.

What about English? I take it books are an index

of culture. In 1956 we published about 12,000 titles, the British published 20,000, and the Russians 30,000. Before television, about 22 per cent of the Americans read, or read in, at least one book a year; today the figure is 17 per cent. As for writing, annual conferences between representatives of business and representative members of the College English Association are devoted to the proposition that the purpose of English studies is better business correspondence and that the purpose is not fulfilled. In *The Educational Forum* for May, 1957, Jesse Bier devotes an article to probing into the causes of errors in freshman composition, including the use of *historical* for *hysterical, unkept* for *unkempt, blaze* for *blasé, course* girl for *chorus* girl, college *carrier* for college *career, sprouse* for *spouse, gentileman* for *gentleman, lassitude* as the opposite of *longitude, Rural Officers Train Corps* as a translation of ROTC, Senators and *Republicans* for Senators and Representatives, and, purest gem of all, *pancreas* for *panacea.* Perhaps there is no general pancreas for the situation, but I cannot but reflect that this sort of thing happens in a country in which libraries, public and academic, are miracles of accessibility. Unfortunately, the latest figures seem to show they are used by only about 10 per cent of the population.

The problem is wider than the efficiency or inefficiency of the secondary schools. A usual requirement for the B.A. degree is one or two years of a modern foreign language. How many students have any command of the foreign language they have thus studied? A common requirement for the doctorate is a reading knowledge of two modern foreign languages, but I need not comment on the sorrowful inability of three-fourths of the candidates for this degree to read any language whatever. The tale is depressing, and I shall not add to the encircling gloom by discussing either the style of doctoral dissertations or the English of comic strips or the curious inability of even mature students to comprehend that ten years, say, from 1660 to 1670 is just as long a time as the ten years which brought them through high school and college into the beginning of a third year of graduate study.

Confronted with deficiencies of this sort, the impatient citizen is likely to exclaim: Let them work harder! Let them study more! Make them more diligent in the schools! Well, diligence is a very good thing, provided it is properly applied, but

mere diligence will not solve a cultural problem
unless the diligence is intelligently directed toward a philosophical end. It is, indeed, the failure
of many good people to understand this truth
that leads to ignorant attacks on universities, colleges, high schools, and so on, as too soft, too easy,
or too vague. This unintelligent attitude can be
found in the current demand that the schools
"tighten up" and start delivering more scientists
and engineers to government and industry. Tighten
up what? The central issue, I suggest, is not tighten-
ing up, nor is it our national ability to create
annual outputs of scientists and engineers or any
other sort of specialist; the central issue is our
national attitude toward learning as a part of
culture.

I have defined learning as humane learning, and
I have said that humane learning includes both
knowledge of and knowledge about the arts. I suggest that one root of our difficulty is the general
assumption that these two kinds of knowledge are
inherently antagonistic, and not, as in fact they
are, complementary. The result is our inability to
realize that every art (like every science) has its
grammar and that until the grammar of the art

is mastered, the meaning of the art cannot be understood. And although Montaigne tells us that the greater part of the world's troubles is due to questions of grammar, it is not grammar in the philological sense that I have chiefly in mind.

Grammar as a philosophic concept means a body of basic statements of fact about any subject, together with a set of rules, practices, or principles governing activity in the field. This is the meaning of grammar I shall employ. It refers at once to a kind of science and to a kind of practice or art, and the two components are clearly basic in most human activities. When, for example, in 1642 Thomas Fuller in his *Holy and Profane State* writes that "manly sports are the grammar of military performance," or when in 1870 Cardinal Newman publishes his *Grammar of Assent,* or when in 1945 Kenneth Burke brings out his *Grammar of Motives,* the writer employs "grammar" in the philosophical sense. Thus Mr. Burke is interested in analyzing the basic forms of thought we use when we attribute motives to man (an analysis of fact) . But he is not content to treat them as passive forms; he is interested in the dynamism of expression involved (the set of principles governing activity). Cardinal Newman in his famous treatise analyzed the situation or situations which lead somebody to accept as true what is presented to him for belief; but Newman concurrently examined the living operations of the mind when it does so.

Even the quaint statement by Thomas Fuller has this dynamic element in it, for it appears in a chapter giving rules for keeping healthy. Recreation he defines as "a second Creation," and his interest is in the action involved in or flowing from forms of recreation. "Those are the best recreations," he finds, "which besides refreshing enable, at least dispose, men to some other good ends. Bowling teaches mens hands and eyes Mathematicks and the rules of Proportion; Swimming hath sav'd many a mans life, when himself hath been both the wares and the ship; Tilting and Fencing is warre without anger; and manly sports are the Grammar of Military performance." The dynamic element in grammar is here, I think, obvious. Grammar leads directly through mastery to delight. Or, put another way, the end of grammar is delight in form.

What do I mean by delight in form? Let me

give a homely illustration. Imagine a young man on a chilly afternoon in October running rapidly a short distance, then plunging with all his weight against a stuffed and heavy bag suspended from a crossbar, and bringing the bag down with him as he sprawls heavily in the dirt. Imagine him picking himself up and walking back whence he started, to repeat the performance time and time again. Imagine ten, fifteen, twenty, thirty, or forty other young men doing the same thing for many afternoon hours. Nothing seems more futile. Parsing an English sentence is by comparison a breathless drama. Yet the young man is glad to repeat this performance endlessly, and what he does is watched gravely and critically by older men, who comment not so much upon his success in pulling the bag off the crossbar, as on the style or form in which he does it. This is known as coming out for the team.

The probabilities of the young man's performing this feat before a large and enthusiastic public audience are uncertain. In the first place it may be said of football that many are called and few are chosen; and in the second place even if he is chosen, he may have no opportunity to bring down an opponent in just this way. Nevertheless, the coaching staff is right in demanding endless practice in this or any other element in football form. Only when form has been so mastered as to pass virtually into the unconscious mind has the young man achieved the goal the coach has set for him. The young man, though he does not know it, is mastering the grammar of his art.

We take all this with becoming seriousness, just as we take similar training seriously in track, or swimming, or tennis, or any other physical art. We do not find it bizarre that an American male who has reached years of discretion spends a good many hours in his backyard swinging a golf club over his head and bringing it down to the turf in a beautiful arc and with a classical precision of timing. On the contrary, we who rate players by form, applaud. We believe we cannot make good golf players, or skaters, or runners, or baseball players, until we have trained them to a sense of form—that is, to effortless and almost unconscious mental and muscular control of the grammar of the sport. We insist, indeed, that complete delight is impossible until this grammar is mastered, and we equally insist that the mastery of grammar is itself a delight. No amateur practicing golf or tennis or swimming but returns from his workout in a glow of virtue, happiness, and perspiration. Everybody approves.

When, however, the issue concerns those arts we include among the humanities, we find, with one exception, that this situation is turned upside down. The mastery of grammatical form not only is not regarded as essential to delight, but grammar in this sense is looked upon as a great bore unnecessarily imposed from above by tradition-ridden, narrow-minded pedants out of sympathy with youth, radicalism, and progress. Why grammar in any shape? Why pause to analyze the structure of literary form in writing, the structure of the sentence in reading, the gross anatomy of the human figure in painting, the principles of proportion and color harmony in decoration, the elements of voice, gesture, posture, and movement in acting? A Stanislavsky begins rehearsals of Gorki's *The Lower Depths* at the Moscow Art Theatre in early summer and produces the play the following December, taking six months in all; when John Barrymore produced *Hamlet,* the cast rehearsed about nine weeks. It is our national habit to speed things up.

The one exception to the general attitude about grammar in the arts seems to be music. In that area we still insist upon mastering finger-work, scales, and the production of competent tones from voice or instrument, largely, I assume, because the production of noises by the unskilled creates a cacophony so distressing, the human ear rebels. I sometimes wish the human eye would rebel with equal vigor.

Now I think there is no single cause that explains why as a people we are impatient with the necessity of mastering the grammar of an art and yet insist upon the need of mastering the grammar of a sport. We are of course a sports-loving nation, we are a nation of activists, we are a social-minded nation; and the slow and lonely process, usually carried on indoors, by which the young reader, the young writer, the young painter, and so on, slowly come to master not merely the elements of their art but also the components of its craftsmanship seems tedious and antisocial. Even in the area of music, in which, as I have said, we seem to perform better than we do in most of the other arts, European teachers tend to believe that though American students work hard, they do not work hard enough, or rather, they do not work with that peculiar consecration Continental performers expect as a matter of course from younger aspirants in opera or concert music. Whether this is a just observation may be disputable, but it throws some light on the question of our national psychology.

There is of course another great element in the situation. Despite fine theories to the contrary, most of us go to school to be trained for jobs. Job-training is serious business. Therefore it is that vocational elements in the curriculum, whether in high school or college, command an immediate respect from parent and child alike. Be the course one in stenography or group therapy, soil mechanics or biochemistry, business law or commercial geography, its relation to one's vocation is immediate, and rating one's attainment is therefore not only easier but more personal and dramatic than is possible in the humanities. Literature, philosophy, ethics, painting, music—these powerful names do not stand for immediate powerful forces. We assent to the general truth that the Declaration of Independence and the Constitution of the United States are erected on a particular system of philosophy; but although we see in the

case of Nazi Germany what happens when a nation
adopts a vicious system of philosophy, we do not
really believe that an understanding of the ideas
of Jefferson is half as important as an understanding of the ideas of Secretary Benson or Mr. Reuther
or the personnel director of General Motors. We
may amiably nod our heads in agreement when we
read the famous statement of Fletcher of Saltoun
that he did not care who made the laws for a nation provided he could be allowed to make its
songs; but our agreement is mere notional assent,
not the real assent that Cardinal Newman talks
about.

The arts, the humanities, despite all that educational philosophers rightly tell us about the importance of humane learning, remain perpetually
fringe benefits; they are not part of our intellectual
investment as chemistry or engineering is. We are,
we believe, a practical-minded nation; and albeit
philosophy and the arts and the languages are all
very good things in their way, we say those who
advocate their study never meet a payroll and
those who practice them never seem to make much
money in the stock market.

I think our national attitude is somewhat changing, as, indeed, it must change in a world split by two philosophies—the Russians' and our own—but my description is still tolerably exact. It is true that among our ideals is the pursuit of happiness, and I have just finished describing the delight the lover of some particular sport discovers in mastering the elements of his hobby. Perhaps it is in the concept of happiness, indeed, that the issue is joined.

I believe it was Frederick the Great who, watching the efforts of the Emperor Joseph II of Austria to modernize his empire, remarked that the trouble with him was that he always took the second step before he took the first. Nationally speaking, we fall into the like error in the field of the arts. We want the happiness that arises from them, but we do not first pause to inquire how we are to establish the basis of durable satisfaction in any one art. It is in vain to tell us, as we might have been told in the days when moral saws were prevalent in copybooks, that there is no democratic road to learning any more than there is that royal road to geometry which King Ptolemy of Egypt demanded of Euclid. We are determined to take the second step without bothering about the first. This queer habit of mind is produced, I think, by various forces in our culture.

One of these components is flattering to the arts. We universally agree that chemistry is hard work, and we expect students to grind away at it, just as we expect them to grind away at engineering. We cannot afford to have prescriptions filled by druggists whose knowledge of pharmacy is as vague as their capacity to write English, just as we cannot afford to have bridges built by engineers whose mastery of stresses and strains in materials is as vague as their mastery of spelling. Preparation for vocation or profession is therefore hard and demanding. The medical student or the future lawyer is so wrapped up in his studies that we have a certain degree of pride in saying that John never leaves the medical school until six o'clock and Joe is in the law school library until ten. We admire and we deplore this rigor. We admire it because it keeps American technology on top of the world; we deplore it because it is narrowing, and at this point we invoke the arts as a medicine against narrowness. Students are encouraged to take courses in literature on the ground that if they don't read literary masterpieces now, they will never read them hereafter—one of the most curious arguments for art I have ever heard. And in general, courses in the humanities are called upon by planners of programs in professional education to undo the damage which plans of professional education have done.

But difficulties arise. The first is that if the whole bent of a student's training, or four-fifths of that training, is in the direction of mastering highly specialized techniques, you cannot, as an annex or an afterthought, for one-fifth of his time somehow expect him to abandon the habits of thought that are the very pith and marrow of his professional training and simultaneously get up a quite different set of habits for the study of the humanities. If the pressure upon the student is, so to say, to learn how to solve problems by the use of a slide rule, he is bewildered when, confronted by a problem in literature or philosophy or painting, you tell him that not the slide rule but the written or spoken word is the instrument he is now expected to use. He is likely to take the position that since he is not clever with words, the problem is beyond him, or that since the problem is not soluble in his terms, it is essentially a frivolous problem. The harassed instructor has then to make an impossible choice: Either he flunks our young engineer or medical student or chemist; or he lowers his standards to the point where most of the engineers, medical students, and chemists can get by. Neither solution promises any mastery of the grammar of the art in question, and therefore both fail to produce any lasting basis of satisfaction in the art.

I am far from saying that young engineers, medical students, and chemists are unintelligent. On the contrary, they commonly exhibit a high order of intelligence, but the intelligence is of a particular sort used for particular ends; and any one who, like myself, has ever undertaken to teach the humanities to engineers will, I think, agree that the problem is not one of intelligence, but one of making the arts appear as something more than a meaningless or an agreeable diversion, a vacation from the real purpose of going to school.

Another anomaly appears. Told that he is to study literature or music or philosophy or some other department of humane learning for the purpose of broadening his knowledge of human nature, the undergraduate naturally expects results—the same kind of measurable results he finds in passing from elementary chemistry to an advanced course. The study of literature does, indeed, increase our knowledge of human life, but it does so in slow, indirect and almost invisible ways, so that when the student from the college of commerce, required to take a course in literature, puts the practical question, "How is the reading of *Hamlet* going to help me as a salesman?" he puts a question that from his point of view makes perfect sense and from the point of view of the instructor in the humanities displays an appalling ignorance.

What, indeed, is the connection between being a sales representative for, say, a lumber company and the required reading of Shelley? When you put the question in these terms, the only honest answer is that there is no connection whatsoever. But the reason the question is framed as it is by the bewildered student is evident enough: He is trying to fuse what I may call the grammar of literary art with what I may call the grammar of vocational or professional training. Out of his unconscious unwillingness to master the elements of an art he is trying to secure the same kind of satisfaction he felt in his sense of mastery of the elements of commercial lore. He is, in sum, like many another honest lad, confused between the claims of knowing an art and knowing about an art. I suspect that our eagerness to use the arts as a specific or a therapeutic to cure educational malformation may lie at the bottom of student confusion in this regard.

Illuminating as an analysis of the use of the humanities for medicinal purposes thus proves to be, I suggest that a still more characteristic difficulty is found in our confusion of the arts with self-expression. The doctrine of self-expression is in one sense simplicity itself; in another sense it is the result of so complex a set of variants that one despairs of analyzing them, and therefore I shall not try. The theory is a legacy from the romantic movement. It holds not only that every individual is unique, it holds also that he cannot be whole or happy until and unless he somehow objectifies his emotional nature through some form of self-created art. Self-expression cannot in this sense take place in science, inasmuch as the ideal of scientific impersonality defeats the attempt; and self-expression must therefore find its outlet in the arts, including sports, for the lack of any other channel.

By definition our technological culture, according to one theory, is supposed to starve or kill individuals. In its crudest form the argument runs that business or industry by confining the worker to meaningless repetitive tasks—the symbol here is the famous nut-tightening routine of Charley Chaplin in the film *Modern Times* (1935)—reduces him to an automaton; and in its more recent formulation, as in Orwell's *1984*, the doctrine holds that cunning manipulation of psychology can produce the faceless and obedient robots of that disturbing book. Social therapy requires that to oppose those tendencies we must encourage the individual to express his own views, his own urges, his own dreams, his own ideals; and since these are highly personalized expressions, he and we must turn to art. Hence it is that from finger-painting in the kindergarten to adult education courses in creative writing an enormous educational activity encourages self-expression. This doctrine is further strengthened by the claim that so-called barbarians and children are "natural artists," as witness in the one case the weaving of Navajo rugs and the shaping of African sculpture, and in the other the innocent charm of juvenile drawings and paintings in the school gymnasium show, suggestive of the later work of Paul Klee.

Nobody wants to stop the pleasures of finger-painting, rhythm bands, folk dancing, and juvenile verse. One can cite the high authority of Plato for the theory that some experience of the arts is necessary for a well-rounded life, and the high authority of Friedrich Schiller to the effect that art is play. But we are once again confusing knowledge of an art and knowledge about an art. The Navajo weaving his beautiful rugs is practicing a craft requiring traditional *expertise* and in that sense is an artist and should be praised; but when we call Goethe or Beethoven or Rodin or Rembrandt an artist we mean that he has passed beyond craftsmanship into philosophy. Neither finger-painting nor a Navajo rug struggles with the riddle of the painful earth. Neither play, however invigorating, nor craftsmanship, however excellent, is in itself synonymous with the arts as the humanities understand the significance of the arts: to give us a reading of life as it has appeared to some of the finest and most subtle minds the race has ever seen. To confuse the self-expression possible to happy play or unhappy adolescence with an understanding of the profound truth that art requires, as Rossetti said of good poetry, fundamental brainwork is to reduce the grammar of any art and of all the arts to mere emotional vaporings.

Let me cite in this context the speech of the French novelist Albert Camus in accepting the Nobel Prize in Stockholm last year.* He said: "I cannot live as a person without my art. And yet I have never set that art above everything else. It is essential to me, on the contrary, because it excludes no one and allows me to live, just as I am, on a footing with all. To me art is not a solitary delight. It is a means of stirring the greatest number of men by providing them with a privileged image of our common joys and woes. Hence it forces the artist not to isolate himself; it subjects him to the humblest and most universal truth. And the man who, as often happens, chose the path of art because he was aware of his difference soon learns that he can nourish his art, and his difference, solely by admitting his resemblance to all. The artist fashions himself in that ceaseless oscillation from himself to

* Albert Camus. *Speech of Acceptance upon the Award of the Nobel Prize for Literature Delivered in Stockholm on the 10th of December 1957.* Translated by Justin O'Brien. New York: Alfred A. Knopf, Inc., 1958.

others, midway between the beauty he cannot do
without and the community from which he cannot tear himself. This is why true artists scorn
nothing. . . . By the same token, the writer's function is not without arduous duties. By definition
he cannot serve today those who make history; he
must serve those who are subject to it. Otherwise
he is alone and deprived of his art. All the armies
of tyranny with their millions of men cannot people his solitude—even, and especially, if he is will-
ing to fall into step with them. But the silence of
an unknown prisoner subjected to humiliations at
the other end of the world is enough to tear the
writer from exile, every time at least that he man-
ages, amid the privileges of freedom, not to forget
that silence, but to relieve it, making it re-echo by
means of art . . . in all the circumstances of his
life, unknown or momentarily famous, the writer
can recapture the feeling of a living community
that will justify him. But only if he accepts as com-
pletely as possible the two trusts that constitute the
nobility of his calling: the service of truth and the
service of freedom. . . . His vocation is to unite
the greatest possible number of men. . . ."

How remote in the light of this profound cry

of the heart seems all our talk about art as therapeutic, art as correction, art as play, and art as
self-expression—particularly art as self-expression!
For art as self-expression begins by denying the
claims of that community of men between whom
and beauty the artist ceaselessly oscillates. It not
only denies, it wipes out all thought of such community. Art as self-expression is nakedly solipsistic.
It cries and cries, a whimpering voice in an empty
universe. The owner of the voice has learned something about art, but of the function of art he knows
little. "What does your painting mean?" we ask
him in all good faith. "Why," he tells us, "it says
what it means, it expresses *me*." "What does this
poem of yours say?—I don't quite understand it."
"Ah, you don't? How stupid of you! It expresses
me, and therefore the blame is entirely upon your
head if you do not comprehend me. Let M. Camus
talk about oscillating between beauty and humanity if he must; I am too much preoccupied with my
own sensibility to trouble about either his unknown prisoner or his common joys and woes.
M. Camus may mean something by declaring that
he can nourish his difference from other men only
by admitting his resemblance to other men, but

people who win Nobel prizes are always chosen by other men; they become hypocritical. And I— I am I, uniquely myself, I shall express myself, even if, or rather because, nobody understands me."

The profound sense of moral responsibility which rings out in M. Camus's address is part and portion of that grammar of art we are too impatient to master. His is the same seriousness of moral purpose that the scientist strives for—that sense of responsibility to the race, which strikes down pseudo-science, however attractive, and insists that physicists and pharmacologists, geologists and engineers, shall be rigorously trained because society cannot afford to have them trained any other way. We shall not get very far in comprehending the relation of art in America to the national welfare until we realize that what is true of the scientist is true of the artist also. The lives of men as various as Turner, Balzac, Beethoven, Rembrandt, Mozart, da Vinci, Millet, Picasso, Caruso, and Milton cry out against our desultory and casual notion that if you learn a little something *about* an art you are therefore equipped with knowledge *of* an art and entitled to all the privileges of poetic license and social irresponsibility.

The grammar of art is more than its components; it is something which begins by trying to understand how these components fuse together into an expression of profound moral responsibility. The elements of art one must learn, just as one must learn scales while singing; but the dynamism of art is the same, in one sense, as the dynamism of football: The player believes that mastery of form brings delight because only through this delight in form can he come to wisdom about the game and, eventually, wisdom about a culture that nourishes such concepts as games, fair play as an ethical rule, and the public responsibility of the players not to play dirty. The ethos of public sports in America is, it seems to me, the fairest product of a tradition that goes back to the Greeks and shares their sense of ethical conduct. Would that we also kept vivid their sense of the equal moral responsibility of the grammar of art!

For it is a mark of our naïveté that when I speak of the moral responsibility of art or when M. Camus speaks of the artist as one who dare not isolate himself from his fellows if he is to remain unique, I shall be accused either of advocating didacticism or of advocating social propaganda. This, however, is to mistake the part for the whole. Didacticism occasionally produces great art, as in a sense it does in *Paradise Lost,* and social propaganda sometimes rises to greatness, as in Picasso's "Guernica" or in the fiction of Dickens attacking the Manchester school of economists; but to confine the aesthetic impact of *Paradise Lost* to its theology and the imaginative power of Dickens to *Hard Times* is a shallow error. When in "Memorial Verses" Arnold wrote of Byron,

> *He taught us little: but our soul*
> *Had felt him like the thunder's roll.*
> *With shivering heart the strife we saw*
> *Of Passion with Eternal Law.*
> *And yet with reverential awe*
> *We watch'd the fount of fiery life*
> *Which serv'd for that Titanic strife.*

he was not concerned for the literary origins of the Byronic hero or the truth of the story that Byron committed incest with his half-sister or the problem of social criticism in *Don Juan;* he was concerned directly with the quality of human energy displayed by a great, if imperfect, spirit, and with the poetical channels through which it found expression. You cannot, twist the matter how you will, discover whether Sophocles would be a socialist, a fascist, a democrat, or a communist, were he alive today; nevertheless the *Œdipus* and the *Antigone* continue to haunt our memories precisely because they oscillate between beauty and the community of men—because, in short, they are simultaneously expressions of truth and expressions of freedom, as science also is.

Just as we must distinguish between science and scientific hardware, between the philosophic mind and the technologist, between the vision of a Newton, a Darwin, and an Einstein and the graduates of a good technological course in civil engineering, so must we learn to distinguish between art and artisanship, between the philosophic vision and the crowd of little men who mistake craftsmanship for illumination and who do not or cannot understand M. Camus when he speaks of the artist perpetually oscillating between beauty and the community of men. Delight in form is possible only when we apprehend what form is to be used for; this is what Arnold and Camus are telling us; and it is this apprehension of the context of training and use that needs to reappear in the arts as a part of humane learning. Even with Freud's winged chariot ever at our ears, it is too late in point of cultural time to go back to the romantic theory of the lonely ego; yet it is precisely backward that the modern doctrine of self-expression wants to lead us today.

3 *"A Joy Forever"*

In these reflections on learning I have hitherto spoken as humanists too often do, as if the fault in achieving a just recognition of the importance of the arts in our culture were always the fault of somebody else. Perhaps, however, scholarship itself is at fault. Perhaps the significance of the arts to the national culture, however defined, is not sufficiently recognized by scholarship; or perhaps the approach of scholarship to the arts as part of higher education is itself misguided. Let us therefore look at the development of scholarship in America and ascertain whether, by tracing its alterations, we can arrive at any clearer notion of the function of the humanities, notably the arts, in American life.

In the United States humane learning has undergone three great transformations. These have been its classical phase, its Germanic phase, and its present analytical phase. Formal learning reached our shores during the seventeenth century in the late afternoon of the European Renaissance. An adventurer like Captain John Smith and more God-fearing persons like William Bradford of Plymouth and Governor Winthrop of Massachusetts were products of that great age which gave us Milton, Bacon, Harvey, and the rest. In the writings of Smith one can detect echoes of the spacious prose of great Elizabeth. Bradford and Winthrop, like the race of seventeenth century clergymen, were learned men in the sense that Milton was a learned man. The center of their learning was the classical tongues, together with Hebrew, and the frame of reference for this learning was not merely the soberer parts of Greek and Latin thought but also that vast body of neo-Latin in which as late as the

time of Newton scholars and scientists communi-
cated with each other. Education was inconceivable
without the study of Latin; and though we may
suspect that John Smith's classical learning was
schoolboy culture, the New England clergyman of
the seventeenth century knew his languages thoroughly and well.

The supremacy of the classics continued into
the eighteenth century as the core of humane
learning. Despite the attacks of Benjamin Franklin, knowledge of the ancient world continued to
be the *sine qua non* of polite education. Indeed,
more than politeness was involved. The very nature of the republic owes much to the thought of
the Ancients. Whether or not it be true that the
members of the Continental Congress could, if
necessary, converse in Latin, there is no doubt of
the profound influence of ancient history and of
classical political theory as well as modern political
theory deriving from it, upon the thought of the
founding fathers. John Adams of Massachusetts
is a case in point. The great debate about the
nature of the state, the rights and duties of citizens,
the lawfulness of resistance, and the theory of representative government assumed as a matter of

course that the participants would make constant reference to the history of the Greek city states and of the Roman republic; and when they wanted an example of the evils of monarchy, all they had to do was to turn to Suetonius's *Lives of the Caesars* for a pertinent instance. Living or recent authorities like Montesquieu founded their discussion of political science upon the same historical basis; and the history of more modern republics like Florence and Geneva was adjudged in the light of classical experience.

If such were the grave and public uses of classical learning, its private and more informal appeal was to be seen in the neo-classical verse of the American eighteenth century (nowadays tedious to us), as well as in the concept of a retired happiness which led many an American gentleman, including Washington and Jefferson, to dream of repeating on the Schuylkill, the Potomac, or at Monticello, the Epicurean happiness of Horace at his Sabine farm.

The achievement of independence did not alter the tradition. At the opening of the nineteenth century, indeed, the vitality of the classical tradition was strengthened by forces from abroad. In Great Britain, in the midst of the romantic movement, there was a classical revival occasioned, among other matters, by excitement over the excavations at Herculaneum and Pompeii and by the arrival in London of the Elgin marbles, noticed by Keats in a famous sonnet. For Americans not of the conservative party, the French Revolution seemed to revive the glories of republican Greece and Rome. The various Revolutionary governments and, eventually, the Directory, the Consulate, and the Empire patterned themselves in one way or another upon the ancient world. Classical furniture was made fashionable for ladies draped in classical garments. The term "Citizen" came from Rome, the golden bees on Napoleon's royal robes were Virgilian bees, and the eagles to which he rhetorically referred on crucial occasions were the eagles of the legions. We too adopted the eagle, which has come permanently to rest on the Great Seal of the United States; and our Greek Revival in architecture echoed in brick, stone, and wood the Hellenism of Keats. With what could we replace classicism? We had as yet developed nothing.

But a difficulty appeared. In Europe classicism was being continually reinvigorated by new scholarship, new interpretation, new philosophical outlooks, new poetic treatment. Consider, as examples, the Helena episode in Goethe's *Faust,* the histories of Greece by Grote, Thirlwall, and others, the exquisite classical scholarship of the French, and eventually a book like Nietzsche's *The Birth of Tragedy.* But this country could produce no burning enthusiast like Winckelmann, no excavator like Schliemann, no historian like Mommsen, no great Platonist or Aristotelian, no metaphysician competent to revivify the meaning of Stoicism as in our time Reinhold Niebuhr has revivified Christian theology. We paid decent tribute to the ancients by naming our cities Sparta, Rome, Athens, Syracuse, Corinth, and so on, and we thought up clumsy coinages like Indianapolis to unite the classical and the barbarian worlds; we housed our legislatures and our banks in classical temples; and we retained Latin on our college diplomas. But the history of the Ancients seemed to us something far away and long ago; the philosophic wisdom of Socrates or Lucretius, the imaginative splendor of Sophocles and Homer, had little influence upon American writing. We "taught" the classics, but that was virtually all we did, and we taught them by that worst of all pedagogical

devices, the rote method. Read the autobiographies
of those who went to college before the Civil War.
Homer and Horace were commonly something to
parse, mere exercises in language. It is symbolical
of the period that that ambitiously named creek,
the Tiber, disappeared from the District of Columbia, and nowadays no inhabitant of Washington can tell you where it ran.

Change came with the adoption of an evolu-
tionary philosophy a little after the middle of the
last century. Everything was now to be studied in
the light of origin and development. The source
of American democracy was sought, not in ancient
Greece and Rome, but in the alleged beginnings
of the New England town meeting amid the dim
forests of prehistoric Germany. Theories of racial
destiny were solemnly proclaimed by American historians. Francis Parkman took Canada away from
the French and gave it to the British, largely because the French were Latin, Mediterranean, and
Catholic, whereas the British were Anglo-Saxon,
Northern, and Protestant; and Theodore Roosevelt
won the West from the remaining French for the
same reason.

The general movement was backward in time to

origins; and as in the nature of the case Latin and Greek were but way-stations in the development of language since the creation of Sanscrit, philologians sought to recreate a mythical Aryan speech, the language of a mythical *Urvolk,* the noble Aryans. In place of studying Homer and Horace graduate students spent endless hours on Old English, Old Norse, Old High German, Gothic, Old French; and the glories of literature were obscured by the toil of tracing sound changes through the linguistic system and identifying gemination and rhotacism wherever they occurred. Nor was this all.

How could you understand a work of art unless you knew how it came into being? This was the question the German scholars asked. Works of literary merit were especially susceptible to the genetic approach, but the various states of an etching, preliminary sketches for a landscape in oil, early and tentative casts for a sculptured head, or early jottings for a symphony were also valuable data.

The art of literature particularly exhibited the strength and weakness of the genetic approach. The business of scholarship was to ascertain who

wrote the work, at what period of his life, in what
circumstances, for what purpose, and with what
immediate or far-reaching results in the way of repute, vogue, or influence. Answering these inquiries involved or created a greater exactness in biog-
raphy than had earlier been common, as well as
searching studies into the intellectual, social, and
political environment surrounding the creator and
the work: Masson's enormous life of Milton is a
prodigious example of this approach.

Then, having ascertained the external environment of the work, the scholar turned to its internal
environment, that is, to its genesis, its composition,
its growth, its revisions. Inheriting from earlier
scholarship reverence for textual exactitude, the
new Germanic scholarship subjected texts to more
severe scrutiny than ever before. The scholar
sought in all sorts of places for sources, that is,
for those stimulating occasions, works, or circumstances that seemed to have set the imagination and
the memory of the artist in motion. He sought to
assemble whatever remained of preliminary studies, sketches, and drafts; he studied these, he dated
them, he placed them in genetic order. He re-
curred to the original manuscript if he could find

it, or to the corrected galley proof, or, at least, to
the original edition, if it was a printed book. In
all this he hoped to shed light upon the meaning,
beauty, and significance of art, as, indeed, he fre-
quently did: Witness Calvin Thomas's great edition of *Faust,* Kittredge's contributions to our
knowledge of Shakespeare, and, in another field,
that noble monument of scholarship, Thayer's life
of Beethoven.

Where evidence was missing, he sought to infer
it as a paleontologist infers the skeleton of an animal from a few remaining bones. The method of
parallel passages proved fruitful. Sometimes the
scholar demonstrated that an unintelligible passage made sense if you consulted other passages in
other works. Sometimes he demonstrated the
probability that such-and-such a work, hitherto
ascribed to A, was really written by B. Sometimes
he showed that what seemed to be original was not
original at all. A kind of universal detective frenzy
came over humanistic learning, as source-hunting,
the heaping up of parallels, the redating of works,
and the breaking of texts into component parts by
various hands became familiar occupations in research. The model was commonly the impeccable

patience of the German *Gelehrter,* who, always
scrupulous in regard to textual accuracy, accepted
with gratitude a theory that gave him the responsibility of making learning as objective and fault-
less as any branch of laboratory science.

We owe an enormous debt to this generation
of scholars. They sorted out manuscripts; they established bibliographical canons; they ascribed the
right works to the right authors; they dated literary
productions; they enabled us to read what the
author wrote and not what somebody else thought
he ought to have written; and they brought to bear
upon the interpretation of masterpieces all sorts
of relevant information as well as much that now
seems to us petty. But their great achievement re-
mains: They turned scholarship from an avocation
for dilettantes into an occupation for professionals;
they established rigorous methods in the field, and
they were content with nothing less than exhaus-
tiveness.

But they were too remote from art. They moved
further and further away from their essential subject. They treated a poem, a canvas, a musical
score, as if it were not so much the subject of scholarship as the occasion for it. Works of art, whether

made of words, or metal, or stone, or paint, or sounds, were mysteriously transmuted into mere documents, with damaging results to both beauty and the happiness that beauty gives.

Take, as examples, two of the greatest works of Biblical scholarship this country has produced, works that have my entire admiration—Robert Pfeiffer's *Introduction to the Old Testament* and Walter Bundy's *Jesus and the First Three Gospels*. These books are unsurpassed for vast knowledge, patience, accuracy, and humility of mind. They sum up the learning of a thousand years. Inevitably, however, the majesty of the Old Testament and the beauty of the New disappear under the weight of learning; and one has to turn to a book like Arnold's *God and the Bible* or to the writings of a man like Albert Schweitzer to redress the balance. And mark that I say "redress"; for Biblical scholarship is quite as essential to our culture as is either the beauty of holiness or the holiness of beauty. It has its place, and a very great place it is. But we must not mistake knowledge about an art for knowledge of an art—in this case, the art of religion.

The pendulum has since swung in an opposite

direction, and in all the arts criticism has become a surrogate for scholarship. As early as 1910, at Columbia, the late Joel Spingarn, in a celebrated lecture on "The New Criticism," introduced the ideas of Croce to American scholars, and in his famous volume *Creative Criticism* (1917) he sharply divided the work of the critic from the work of the scholar.

A little later I. A. Richards, in *Principles of Literary Criticism* and again in *Practical Criticism,* demonstrated that whatever the values of scholarship, scholarship did not succeed in getting students to read poems with understanding. By and by, T. S. Eliot was to insist that criticism should be concerned with the poem, not with the poet; and John Crowe Ransom, in a book like *The World's Body* (1938), argued that the poet is as good as the scientist in interpreting the world, that poems, when they are successful, give a totality of experience, a kind of systemic knowledge of their own; and that to grasp this experience and this knowledge we must concentrate upon the poem, not upon information about the poem. Mr. Ransom, however, less intransigent than some of his contemporaries, has never denied the worth of scholarship, he has merely subordinated it to what seems to him its proper role as explanation.

While the movement known as the New Criticism was sweeping through graduate departments of English, analogous theories were being developed in the fine arts by critics and theorists like Roger Fry, Clive Bell, and Leo Stein, each of whom insisted in his own way that painting, especially modern painting, expresses nothing but itself and that to seek in it moral or biographical values is to alter or sophisticate the meaning of art.

Musical parallels are perhaps not so clear, but the writing of musical scores of a high degree of complexity usually and exhibiting astonishing feats in atonality and anarchical key relations and rhythmical structure, compositions intended rather for craftsmen than for the public, is in a large, loose way a kind of equivalent.

It is impossible in short space to be just to a movement of this dimension, especially when I do not pretend to understand all its phases, but the general drift seems clear. A poem is not meaning but statement; a painting does not describe, it exists. Statement, existence, imply that the work of art is *there,* is a unique phenomenon added to the phenomenal world through the creativity of the artist as a self-determined end, not as an activity in the service of something else—say, representation or religion, social protest or morality, imitation or nationalism.

In the case of painting not only is "representation" out—that is, the modern painter does not try, as many nineteenth-century painters did, to rival the camera by creating a replica of visual experience—but also any theoretical context for painting as painting vanishes, whatever school or tendency the painter may seem to belong to. Theoretically, at least, the attention of the spectator is supposed to be directed to the exploitation of the medium for its own sake; that is, the expressiveness of a wash or of impasto, of laying color on with a palette knife or dribbling or sprinkling it from a brush, is a statement of what one can do by doing this and not doing something else. Painting may occasion, but it does not express, emotion or thought, just as it may suggest landscape or situation or character without representing any of these traditional themes. Of course I put the extreme case, knowing that even abstract art may take off from memories or observations of the human form, of human artifacts, or of objects in nature. One of the ironic results is of course that if we seek any clue to the puzzle—why this abstract pattern rather than that one—we are forced to consider the psyche of the painter, so that the biographical information that has just been ushered out of the door has to come back by the window as we learn that so-and-so's colors or patterns are as they are because he is a pessimist or a mystic, and so on.

In the study of literature the attention of critics has been concentrated rather more upon poetry than upon prose, albeit latterly a small library of selected novelists has come in for closer scrutiny. Poems, but not long poems and not narrative poems, by a select group of favorite writers, ranging from John Donne to John Crowe Ransom, have been subjected to close textual analysis, and a whole new critical vocabulary has been established, a whole new set of critical postulates has come into being, based in part on depth psychology and in part on philosophies of the irrational. Words such as "symbol," "vision," and "myth," and phrases like "tenor and vehicle," "tension and release," and "density of surface," have taken on special technical meanings. "Modern criticism," writes Professor Mark Schorer, "through its exacting scrutiny of literary texts, has demonstrated with finality that in art beauty and truth are indivisible and one." As a literary historian, I am professionally doubtful that anything is demonstrated with finality, but this is boldly and finely said.

Of course many practitioners of this approach to literary study seem unaware that textual criticism of this kind existed before their time, though a reading of Hyder Rollins's magisterial variorum edition of Shakespeare's sonnets will demonstrate how closely texts have been scrutinized in the past for hidden meanings by generations of scholars. Mr. Schorer goes on to remark: "When we speak of technique, then we speak of nearly everything"; for, he says, "technique is the only means . . . of discovering, exploring, developing [a] subject, of conveying its meaning, and, finally, of evaluating it." I understand and applaud him. But I remember that something of this sort was taught for years as Columbia University by Professor Brander Matthews, whose generation tried to help writers avoid the fogginess of romantic art by disciplining themselves in French literary theory and practice.

These observations, perhaps more mischievous than important, point to a certain lack of historicity in the movement. What is of greater cultural significance are two reproaches brought against the New Criticism: first, that it chokes creativity by all this insistence upon subtlety of meaning; and second, that it has started a kind of civil war between literary criticism and historical scholarship, especially in the graduate schools. The warfare seems to me imaginary. Far from repudiating scholarship, the critics lean upon it for their effects: An example is Mr. Eliot's famous essay on *Hamlet,* which depends for its whole point upon Mr. Eliot's mastery of what scholarship has discovered about the history of the *Hamlet* theme. On the other hand, just as it is the business of criticism to understand a work of art, so scholarship, except in the very dullest hands, has always found some degree of direct interpretive activity a necessary part of its labors, with the result that the problem is one of emphasis rather than of warfare or denial.

But the question of the effect of modern criticism upon creativity is, I think, not to be settled so easily, even though so good a critic as Cleanth

Brooks tries to get around the difficulty by deprecating the use of "Alexandrian" as an epithet to characterize criticism. The business of the critic, he rightly says, is to be as good a critic as he can; his business is to find out how the language in a poem actually works; and when he has done that, he has fulfilled his function. But *has* he fulfilled his whole function?

Let me turn before answering to another field—that of philosophy. My colleague, Professor Morton White, is the editor of an admirable anthology and commentary on recent and contemporary philosophy. This book he entitles *The Age of Analysis;* and the appropriateness of his title springs not only from the vogue and influence of really great thinkers like Carnap, Moore, Wittgenstein, and Bertrand Russell but also from ironical reference to their little imitators. For what has happened in philosophy, at least in England and the United States, is a failure of assertion. Basing their methods in part upon the discoveries of depth psychology and in part upon the subtleties of mathematical and linguistic analysis, modern metaphysicians have turned upon the haziness of general statements the operations of language itself, the dif-

ficulties of communicating anything from A to B,
C, D, and E; and, pursuing these inquiries with
extraordinary diligence, they have preceded and
paralleled literary criticism in a kind of analytical
destruction of whatever is general or broad or taken
for granted. The Abbé Dimnet some years ago
warned us to beware of looking for anything, since
we were sure to find it; and the so-called Oxford
school has been, like the so-called New Criticism,
unusually successful in discovering difficulties in
what before had seemed plain. But with what
general cultural results? Have they fulfilled their
whole duty as philosophers? Let Mr. White answer the question.

In the final pages of his admirable book, Mr.
White pleads for a reunion of the two great
philosophical currents of modern times—the humane and cultivated interests of Continental philosophers and the analytic and linguistic skills
of the Anglo-American school. His own philosophical sympathies, he says plainly, are with the latter
tradition, but he notes the danger in which they
stand: "As long as the custodians of philosophical
technique develop axes with which to sharpen
other axes, they risk developing a sense of weariness

and emptiness in themselves and in those who read them." He concludes his book with this striking sentence: "We live in dreadful times, when a world in conflict seeks and despises that combination of technique and vision for which the great philosophers are justly famous; their successors should not shirk the responsibility to carry on with equal respect for logic and life." Is it not striking that Professor White comes out very much where M. Camus comes out, in his insistence that the grammar of a subject—in this case of philosophy—is something more than an analysis of its parts?

So, too, it seems to me that the analytical critic of the art of literature fails to fulfill all of his function when, as he does in extreme cases, he assumes or seems to assume that hunting down subtleties of meaning is a triumph of insight. He may, indeed, "enrich" some poem by unveiling, in his phrase, various levels of meaning in its words and by uncovering myth and symbol expressive of the unconscious of the author; but he has not thereby necessarily made the poem more attractive or more beautiful or a better stay against confusion.

Humane learning, it seems to me, has as its principal aim the elucidation of what we quaintly call the human predicament, that is, the eternal conflict between the aspirations and the frustrations of man. Its subjects, or rather its companions in this enterprise, are philosophy and art in the widest sense of these two great words. The object of learning is coterminous with the object of philosophy, and the object of art is to seek that stay against confusion, which is joy. I spoke earlier of the happiness that comes from gradually mastering the grammar of any subject, but this happiness cannot come if the skill of the grammarian is exalted above the power of the creator. It is still true that we murder to dissect, important as dissection must always be. The question of the poet, however, is cogent:

> *Think you, 'mid all this mighty sum*
> *Of things forever speaking,*
> *That nothing of itself will come,*
> *But we must still be seeking?*

The profound and elusive truth in Wordsworth's poem is one of the most difficult truths to define and to establish, but until we establish it scholarship leads away from, and not into, the work of art. Books were made for men, not men for books,

and so likewise were paintings, symphonies, build-
ings, philosophy, and scholarship. Poems may be
the occasion for scholarship, but they should never
be merely the excuse for it. Until we realize that
humane learning like the god Janus has two faces,
we shall not understand what learning is and
why its object is joy. Learning is more than information, just as art is more than inspiration. The
scholar gets beyond erudition only when, through
empathy, he learns to participate in the creation
of art; but the artist will not communicate to
anybody save himself unless on his side he learns
that he belongs to culture and that to this culture
(maintained in part by scholarship), in so far as
he is an artist, he is in greater or lesser degree
responsible. Learning is a union of imagination
with fact, the marriage of information and insight,
the fusion of scientific accuracy with a passionate
sympathy for the human predicament. Learning
is about philosophy and the arts; but philosophy
and the arts are also about learning.

I owe my title, *A Joy Forever,* to John Ruskin,
whose writings like huge, abandoned caravels lie
stranded on the shores of Time. It was under this
title that he republished in 1880 the work which

appeared a hundred years ago as *The Political Economy of Art.* This is full of Victorian fallacies, but it is also full of Victorian grandeur, and in it I find this passage: "Observe, there are two great reciprocal duties concerning industry, constantly to be exchanged between the living and the dead. We, as we live and work, are to be always thinking of those who are to come after us; that what we may do may be serviceable, so far as we can make it so, to them, as well as to us . . . each generation will only be happy or powerful to the pitch that it ought to be, in fulfilling these two duties to the Past and the Future. Its own work will never be rightly done, even for itself—never good, or noble, or pleasurable to its own eyes—if it does not prepare it also for the eyes of generations yet to come. And its own possessions will never be enough for it, and its own wisdom never enough for it, unless it avails itself gratefully and tenderly of the treasures and the wisdom bequeathed to it by its ancestors."

Never good, or noble, or pleasurable to its own eyes! Its own possessions will never be enough, its own wisdom never enough, unless it avails itself gratefully and tenderly of the treasures and the wisdom bequeathed by its ancestors! What can be more eminently nineteenth century? And yet is it not precisely in our sense of the continuity of human wisdom and of human joy that we scholars find delight? Erwin Panofsky reminds us that the cosmos of culture, like the cosmos of nature, is a structure in time and space. What the scholar does, he further points out, is not to erect a rational superstructure on an irrational foundation, but to develop his re-creative experiences so as to conform with the results of his archaeological research. Archaeological research is empty without aesthetic re-creation, but aesthetic re-creation is irrational without archaeological research. Why?

I think Professor Panofsky's answer is still the right one: because we are interested in reality. Reality is a function of explanation, and explanation in turn is a function of that contemplation, that pause for understanding which is the joy of learning. Professor Panofsky puts the matter picturesquely when he says: "The man who takes a paper dollar in exchange for twenty-five apples commits an act of faith, and subjects himself to a theoretical doctrine, as did the medieval man who paid for an indulgence. The man who is run over by an automobile is run over by mathematics, physics, and chemistry." "It is impossible," he concludes, "to conceive of our world in terms of action alone."

Another distinguished critic of art, Bernard Berenson, points out that learning enables us to appraise objects and artifacts according to their significance: first as to the degree that they enable us to reconstruct the past in general, then to reconstruct the history of a given art, and finally to select and interpret the history of the past which can still vitalize and humanize us. The end of such learning is to seek out "the life-enhancement that results from identifying oneself with the object or putting oneself in its place." His description of this process is too technical for me to quote it here, and he talks principally about historians of art; yet what he says applies in equal measure to the general field of learning. Its purpose is to find the life-enhancing values.

I am, then, persuaded that learning forever has two aspects: the aspect of knowledge *about,* and the aspect of knowledge *of;* that is to say, scholarly information and imaginative empathy. Fused into a harmonious whole, learning is one of the durable satisfactions of life—the joy that arises from the sense of participating in the totality of human experience.

Learning, however, may be travestied in opposite ways. One of these travesties is pedantry—the form of learning without its spirit—and with pedantry we are all supposed to be familiar. The other travesty is, I think, wider spread, less understood, and more difficult to identify. I shall call it appreciationism. It is that approach to art and philosophy which mistakes emotion for insight, the emotion being forever sentimental. Such emotion makes no demand on the individual, matures nobody, offers no challenge to the intellect, and invariably fails us in any crisis. Its transient pleasures are without results upon character, whatever they may do for personality. It is an attempt to teach without intellect, which is supported by the doctrine that even a naïve acquaintance with great minds is better than no acquaintance at all. Perhaps. But do we also hold that a child's notion of electricity is sufficient for the citizen of the atomic age? If this seems to you an extreme or misleading parallel, I remind you that a child's notion of ancient history furnished the drive behind Mussolini's pasteboard empire and that an even more infantile notion of philosophy and biology lay behind the lurid massacres of Hitler's time.

Scholarship like science is difficult; learning like the theory of science is even more exacting; and acquiring a humane point of view is one of the supreme achievements of the mind. I see no more reason to suppose that most of us can rise to the stature of a Goethe or a Burckhardt than to suppose that most of us can rise to the stature of a Darwin or an Einstein. The searching experience, the subtle ideational processes, the revelatory glories of a Beethoven, a Shakespeare, a Michelangelo, a Thomas Aquinas, are not for the holidays of the intellect, are not a sort of external plaster to be applied when the serious work of science is done for the day and all we want is a little vacation. The humanities are vast and demanding. If the biologist seeks to solve the riddle of the painful earth, so do the metaphysician and the poet. Precisely as the joy of chemistry is not to do parlor tricks but to understand the constitution of matter, so the joy of learning is not the ability to solve crossword puzzles and win money on television shows but the capacity to think greatly of man and about him and of the arts that best express him.

Does all this mean that learning is so difficult we should not attempt it in the schools? As well say that because physics is difficult, we should not there attempt it. We do not think that the aim of elementary physics is a vague, pleasant emotion; why then should we think that poetry is merely emotion? We simply cannot be satisfied with an emotional concept of learning, even at elementary levels. Learning is or should be something vital, affirmative, intelligent, and bracing—not the possession of the cultist or the pedant, not the possession of the sentimentalist any more than biology or algebra is to be sentimentally conceived. The concern of learning is with wisdom, with the maturities of thought, with language as the form of thought; and its disciplines must, like the disciplines of science, be exacting. Its aim is comprehension, and in comprehension there lives for those who can catch some glimpse of it a bracing and eternal joy.